YES, LORD

YES,
LORD

Dona Hoffman

Publishing House
St. Louis   London

Cover and body photos
by Harold Hoffman

Concordia Publishing House, St. Louis, Missouri
Concordia Publishing House Ltd., London, E. C. 1
Copyright © 1975 Concordia Publishing House

MANUFACTURED IN THE UNITED STATES OF AMERICA

Library of Congress Cataloging in Publication Data

Hoffman, Dona, 1932-
    Yes, Lord.

    Includes correspondence between the author and Paul G. Bretscher.
    1. Suffering. 2. Consolation. 3. Hoffman, Dona, 1932-
4. Bretscher, Paul G. I. Bretscher, Paul G. II. Title.
BV4909.H6   242'.4   74-30867
ISBN 0-570-03195-8

To Pastor "George" (the late Rev. A. L. Hillmann)
    who showed me that because of Jesus
    I am no longer a wanderer
To Pastor Paul
    who is unafraid of my doubts and my failings
    and who teaches me about God's upside-down gifts
To Pastor Bob
    who gives new meaning to the word *joy*
And to every God's-child
    who has been willing to be
    a channel of God's caring for me

DIGNITY

Listen.

It is the greatest compliment
you can give:

that I am worth hearing.

INTRODUCTION

Most books are written. This one just happened. It wasn't intended — its potential existence was simply discovered. With that kind of discovery comes a sense of wonder at the hand and intention of God.

The book is "written," to be sure. Framed in correspondence, it is augmented by poems enclosed with Dona's letters, by reminiscences from her random diary called the *Journal*, by snippets from a handwritten notebook of thoughts titled *Knock Gently*, by drawings here and there, and by a few of Hal's photographs and Dona's matching poems which they had submitted as a possible book manuscript.

The story is a segment of life, beginning where it must begin and ending at what seems the natural ending. It is therefore not a biography. Within its limits it is the story of Dona, of course, in whom God by the strange humor he calls his "wisdom" invests remarkable gifts, ranging from extraordinary talents to extraordinary sufferings.

But it is more. It is a story of the church, stumbling in its inadequacies, yet catching on to and yearning to use its power, the Word of God. It is God working in the variety of gifts the Spirit has invested in the members of Christ's One Body, including the freedom to be wrong or to be right, "whichever is true," as one of Dona's poems has it. By the power of God's promises, in the love, forgiveness, and mutual encouragement of His people, faith struggles against sight, hope against experience.

11

I first "met" Mrs. Hoffman when a poem of hers appeared in February 1967, to which I was moved to respond. (Subsequently I quoted that poem in my book *The Holy Infection*, Concordia, 1969.) Six months later she replied, enclosing three new poems.

The correspondence continued intermittently for some time, with mutual joy and enrichment. At some point I became "Paul" and Mrs. Hoffman "Dona." The longest lapse in the exchange (a year and a half) ended in April 1972, when I included her in the mailing of a family Easter greeting. In her reply she alluded to an "85% chance" she had cancer.

I prayed the Lord to "give her that other 15%," as He had once given 15 years to Hezekiah. Then came the letter with which this book begins.

Dates, names, and places are all real. But the reality that makes them worth sharing in this way is the halo that covers them all—the love of God in Christ Jesus our Lord.

Paul G. Bretscher

Dear Paul,

At times God says NO. Loudly. Like a slap. I have cancer and (supposedly, but who ever knows?) less than 3 years to live. Sometimes I feel honored to have been given "notice" (after all, life is 100% fatal) so that I may prepare. Other times I feel cheated and troubled. For instance, my husband and I have tried for several years to get a book of poetry-photos published. Does it matter to God that we, too, have a message to share? Oh, I know the answers, but I don't always believe them.

You're right. We don't really know what we want. In the same stretching moment there is both rebellion and euphoria, and now the bewilderment: What *do* I want? I can only commit myself hourly, *minutely*, to Him "who regards our Completion as great an act of His glory as our Creation." That was beautiful, Paul—and just what I needed. I dare not despair. Despair is the greatest blasphemy.

My diet consists of "nothing canned, cooked, or processed; no milk, cheese, or eggs; no vinegar, coffee, chocolate; no peanuts. The cancer victim must give up forever these foods in every form." Do you realize what that means? One ton of lettuce, delivered right to your door! Buying a juicer and throwing away the range. (Stop! What about the family?) The dog standing beside the oven, howling. Seeing 457 TV commercials (do they *have* to?) about roast beef and gravy. Being alive enough to hate lettuce. Marveling how self-discipline and self-pity are brothers.

13

When I opened my Bible after having seen the doctor, I met the words "alive in Christ Jesus," and it struck me how eternity has already begun for the Christian, so that this body—for all its ties to this earth—is neither necessary nor desirable, except as it contains and relates to the Spirit of Life.

Thank you for your letter. And for being *you*.

Dona

SMILE

Want to hear something funny?
When I first got sick
I prayed
    God — don't let it be diabetes!
And He said

        OK.

WALKING THROUGH THE VALLEY

Looking back, I see that I could not write in the Journal during those months because of shock. But, oh, I remember that day! I got home from the doctor and saw our neighbors outside, trimming their lawn. I wanted to run to them and cry, "How can you mow the lawn when I am dying of cancer! I am dying—do you hear? *Do you care?*" Of course they would have cared, but they never knew. It was an awful, sacred secret that by some unspoken law was not to be unburdened upon anyone that day.

But I remember, too, Harold's arms around me, and hearing his warm heart against my ear, and his love trying to reach through to my hurt and cover it over.

I remember telling Dan and Larry. They'd just been confirmed, and Hal had compared it to a Bar Mitzvah. "Behold—now you are men," he had told them in their joy, even as he had told Michael before them. Now Hal held one boy and I the other, and I told them "Now, *now* you are men," because of the sorrow they had to bear. And they seemed to understand the paradox of it, and we wept without shame. We were glad that we had told them, because we all became closer to each other and to God.

I remember that Mike was told gently and calmly, and his eyes showed that he did not accept it, and it was over a week after the others knew before he could be told again, and only then did he comprehend. He wondered why he was the last to know, but of course he wasn't—he was just the last to understand.

Sara came home from college after finals. She had her friend Kathy with her, and we all joked about moving. Then Sara's eye caught mine, and we held one another and cried together. She knew. She and I had waited for the test results, and we remembered how we had laughed at the possibility of cancer. And now we made a pact never again to say, "It can't get worse," because it always did get worse, and to say it was like calling a curse down upon ourselves.

Then we moved, out of mountain country and away from nearly 20 years of friends and music. Out of the green and tall mountains, the beckoning valleys, the unsurpassed and rugged beauty of the Northwest, into the "heart of Dixie."

Journal

1971
December 20
    Our Christmas card:

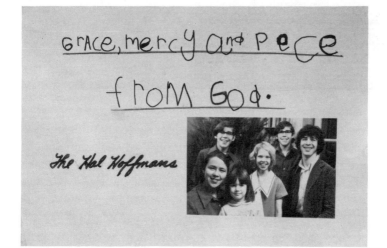

Dear, dear Dona,

Just looked again at the Christmas picture of your children, all so beautiful, and the precious child's hand wishing me "Grace, mercy, and pece." Wish I had a picture of you, or of you and Hal, to go with it. Mostly I wish I could know you all face-to-face, and my family your family, the encounter of frailty with frailty, and yet wearing the halo of divine mercy and promise which secretly makes everything new, free, and full of joy.

Sara is so very pretty — so is Mike and all the rest — but I guess a man notices a girl first as a kind of symbol of everything good in God's creation. And she and Mike are reaching the maturity of stature and appearance which will remain with them with little noticeable change, God willing, for maybe the next 30 years. Can you imagine? When the century turns, they will still be young.

We can't really see that far. We can only project, as computers do, on the basis of present evidences. So I can't help but think and wonder about lettuce, and a stove that dares to share its gifts with some and withhold them from others, and about all the unfairnesses of life that defy our protest because they come from God Himself and not from man's lovelessness and inhumanity to man. And the real test, whether we are abased or whether we abound — can we still fear, love, trust, and hope in our God above anything else? Could Jesus honor his Father on the cross as well as on the fresh and green hills and lakes of Galilee?

But I pray God to give you the grace to be freely human, just as human as you are — to cry freely and explosively when it hits you (think what we would miss if the disciples had never seen Jesus cry!), to be angry when it hits you and not hide it from those who love you—so that your moments of peace, laughter, and tenderness may also be real. The strange treasure God is investing in you now isn't meant just for you, but for family, and your church, and even at so great a distance, also for me. You don't need to think of that, as though to form yourself into some model of self-created behavior. Just be Dona, the Dona who knows the power of sin and temptation but doesn't have to be ashamed or afraid of it because the word of divine promise holds her, even through the dreadful moments when Satan screams that it is all futile and empty. I don't know how it was possible, but Jesus survived his Gethsemane, and you will yours.

> grace, mercy and pece from God,
> Paul

Sept. 1, 1972

Dear Paul,

Your letter was forwarded to me. How can I thank you?
I have read it no less than 2-dozen times. You keep me
centered on Christ, Paul, and oh, I need Him. We have
moved — rather suddenly — to the southeast U. S. Harold's job
was in jeopardy at the shipyard in Seattle. (He microfilms
drawings and documents to Navy specifications.) His
imminent layoff, the news of my malignancy, and the offer
of a job in a shipyard in the South, all came within 3 weeks
of each other. We felt it was God's hand that we move.
Perhaps there is healing for me here. (God knows I don't
want to die here!) Harold commutes every day, 40 miles
one way. I see him hardly at all.

Another dream: The family and I were traveling down
an endless, dark tunnel, which took hairpin curves.
Suddenly the tunnel forked. We took the left side. A small
light came from the wall. I looked closer and saw it was a
barred window. Someone (it was you) *lifted me up* to look out
of it, and I realized we were inside a mountain (the bowels
of the earth, I remember thinking). A Voice told me that
we were now "about 1½ stories, or a time and a half-time"
from our destination: A meadow waited below — sunlit,
green, and peaceful. "We have come a long way in the dark,"
Harold said. I was very tired, but grateful to have seen the
little light. That was the end of my dream.

Three friends (Job's?) — perhaps in their anxiety — insist
that I "try spiritual healing." Surely to place your whole self
into God's hands is the absolute in healing. They wonder,

now, at my faith—because I insist that I must learn to want Christ more than I want healing, that perhaps the latter will follow, but I need a relationship with Him "which is of a calibre uninjured if physical health is not recovered." (Leslie Weatherhead)

How dare I pray for health? If God says no again, so desperate am I, that I might turn from Him. No, I would rather know Him and hear Him call me friend. I'd rather cling to His love for me than take a chance that He and I would be separated. If He wants, He can heal me (and surely they can pray for this). But if He chooses, I shall enter the Greater Healing. Is there any other way?

Besides being very tired, I am also confused, and I find that my mind often does not generate complete thoughts at one time. Perhaps this is evident! I have read Hab. 3:17-19 over and over. We are not abandoned. It is at the "end of the rope" that God becomes real, becomes personal, and the Spirit is able to begin His work.

> Write to me—tell me
> what I must know—
> Dona

HOURS

God
these are heavy hours
upon my shoulders
    old hours come around again
bum hours
looking for a handout.

Dear Dona,

I still wait for the chance to know you and your family face-to-face, to hear the sound of your voice, and to pray with you. Perhaps the Lord will still make it possible.

I had a dream once, about hanging in terror and darkness onto the end of a rope, like yours, getting weaker and yet hanging on, for the rope was my only safety. A voice kept saying, "Let go, my child, don't be afraid; it's all right. Let go, trust me, let go." But I couldn't believe the voice until I was so weak I just couldn't hang on any longer. So I listened in the face of despair and let go. Do you know what happened? I didn't fall at all! The solid ground caught me, only inches beneath my dangling feet. Everything was light and beautiful. The only thing I couldn't see was the rope! That's what repentance means: "Let it all go and come and follow me, and you will have treasures in heaven." But why, why must we be "at the end of our rope" before that Word makes sense to us?

The Lord has taught you so much Dona and yet keeps giving you more. Even while He seems to be taking everything away, He keeps adding to you. "To everyone who has will more be given" (Luke 19:26). How utterly unfair, mysterious, and yet true!

Do you remember when I told you of Marjorie Kelley, her cancer, and the victory she won at Easter 1970? One day she had a visitor in the hospital who offered to have someone blessed with the spiritual gift of healing come and lay hands on her. Marjorie told me about it when I came that afternoon. I don't remember exactly how she answered him—something like, "Thank you, but the Lord has already given me the healing I need, and if He has in mind to do more, He will." "Was that all right?" she asked me. It was a time for tears, but they were sweet tears, with the joy of Jesus in them. "Be of good cheer, I have overcome the world!" Dear God, how wonderfully "all right" You manage to make things!

I keep praying that the Lord will yet overcome the sickness that works in your body, so that your family and church and world will not lose so quickly so dear a gift. The Old Testament lesson for tomorrow is Job 5:17-26, and Pastor Frazell, my assistant, is preaching on "Deliver us from evil": "He will deliver you from six troubles; in seven there shall no evil touch you."

So may the Lord have ready for you new and refreshing drafts of His living water, when those dry days come. It must be so hard, so complicated, so futile — to start life over again as in a strange land. But the Lord will make that good too, and not a moment of it will be forgotten. He knows all your tossings, catches and preserves every tear as something eternally precious in His bottle (Ps. 56:8). *So you trust the secret of time and life to Him who creates both and gives them to us for our joy and His glory.*

No poem with your last letter, except that the whole letter is a poem. Maybe some day you will write your own stanza to the tune of Hab. 3:17-19. I'm sure the Spirit would be delighted.

You are beautiful, Dona, beautiful in your personhood, beautiful in all your human struggle to live out a calling in all those earthbound and captive duties where it is so hard to see any halo, beautiful above all because "the beauty of the Lord our God is upon you" (Ps. 90:17). That's what makes all the rest a part of eternal life.

Richest blessings in Christ,
Paul

24

Dear Paul,

I am — emotionally — much better now. For a while the Great Depression had nothing on me. THAT was only money and food and jobs. . . .

Pastor Bob puts on a good feed. He speaks often about Christian joy. It is true — we are such a sad, somber lot. We need to learn that joy appears only when we look for ways to help others find it.

I keep telling myself it is all right to be tired, to spend much of the day in bed. I still fight guilt. So many ways I could help if I had the energy, so many avenues of beauty to explore. I have to keep handing it all over to God — the guilt, the fatigue, the frustration — worse of all, the regrets for the times I didn't help.

At church Pastor Bob was kind enough to let me try directing a small junior choir for the Reformation service. Sara drives me there. Harold drives me back and does all the phoning. Tami is in charge of pencils. Dan and Larry keep Amy. All I have to do is make it interesting for the kids. It is exhausting, yes. But lovely.

What is it to dream you are dreaming? A voice said (in my dream's dream), *"You will not die of cancer."* I "awoke" and told Harold about it, in the presence of a friend. I don't know why, but I didn't add the words "of cancer" when telling Harold. Therefore the retelling came out "You will not die." The friend commented, "That was a *powerful prayer.*" Then I was truly awake.

That dream occurred the same day you mailed your heartening letter. Could it be a prophecy, or is it fantasy to

25

"dream a dream"? *Dum spiro, spero!*

The South is quite a change from the Northwest—no fresh, constant breezes, no mountains shouldering the sky, no thousand flowers splashing color. Dear God, I am homesick.

Yes, I remember Marjorie Kelley's story very well. Marjorie couldn't have known, but she has helped me so much already. "The garden is full of weeds. . . ."

My Amy is 6 years old now and fairly bright. I kissed her good-night. "You just kissed God," she said. I was incredulous, but kept my cool. "How is that?" I asked. "Because God is in me," she answered. Of course. Of course. It is all so simple. Why don't I remember that?

> I am deeply grateful that you care.
> In love, with the Spirit—
> Dona

Journal

1972
October 10

I had a beautiful dream: Jesus walked by me, and as He did, He handed me a beautiful, pink, long-stemmed rose. Immediately came the interpretation—*Jesus "rose"* from the dead. *Walk with Him who has that power.*

I don't know whether it means I will be healed or that Christians never die. Maybe it is not even prophetic, but the message comes through: Jesus is to be my Lord. It was a peaceful experience.

A letter from the Bakers in Seattle brought tears to my eyes. Happy tears. They offer help in the way of schooling for the two little girls if my healing consists of dying. How I miss my friends!

Paul,

I reread your letter and see I have not answered all the good Word. I am so happy to hear that Marjorie overcame a need for faith healing. She helps me again! It is a terrible blow to one's faith, you know, when Scripture seems to taunt you: "Jesus healed them. . . . Jesus the same yesterday, today." But your *Holy Infection* has turned me around. "God kills and God heals. Blessed be the name of the Lord!"

While I only glimpsed the meaning behind *The Holy Infection* a few years ago, today it is suddenly very clear. It is a beautiful message of leaving all to God. I am grateful to you. If God should choose suffering and death by cancer for me, I not only finally accept it, but I joyfully enter into it, knowing He will provide courage to bear it all. Perhaps today is a mountaintop experience and I am due for a fall, but right now God is very close. I have no trouble loving my family over and through the discomfort because (today at least) He has put His finger upon me — He has touched me and His will is mine. How peaceful and good I feel! How I love Him! I feel — the first time in my *life*, Paul — I feel loved by God.

It was only a few years ago that I was able to feel any kind of love at all. Before that I was able to give it (but even to give had to be God working in me: I knew that). Never received it, even from my kids, and I thanked God that I was not insane. (Harold had serious doubts about THAT.) Then on Sept. 5 I got the flu, and I was lying there on the couch, wondering, "What will Harold do when he gets home? Will he care? *Of course he will care!*" I had never before experienced the feeling that someone would truly be concerned about me. I wept copious tears of self-pity and wonder and joy and—apprehension: What if I were wrong?

It was a long, long childhood to have to overcome. Anyway, I mulled it over in my mind: He will be surprised to see me lying here on the couch. He will probably come and kneel down and say, "Honey, what's wrong? Can I get you anything?"

As the clock approached 5:30, I became more and more nervous, for if he behaved as I felt he might, then I would know love! You see? At last I could recognize it and therefore receive it. It was so important to *know*. Harold finally got home, and when he saw me, he kneeled beside me and he said, *"Honey, what's wrong? Can I get you anything?"*

And now God's saying, "Child! Can I give you anything?" And it is enough that He is *there*, beside me. Who needs anything else?

> I had to tell you!
> Abundantly, with joy—Dona

Journal

1972
October 15

Pain. You discover "how great is the capacity for that sensation" (John Muir, 1911). I have also discovered that yoga, while it overcomes pain, transcends consciousness too, and then I am no longer a mother, just a body with a transcendent consciousness. There must be another way. . . .

October 22

Today brought our official welcome into our new church. How is it possible for one moment to be at once so sad and so beautiful?

October 23

A new test determines the lack of minerals, or mineral imbalance, in the system. The test consists of examining under a microscope some hair from the back of your head, close to the scalp. The kids roll over in hysteria every time they are behind me.

PATTERNS

Do you make plans?
    I am done with plans.
Do you set goals?
    I have relinquished them.
Do you announce schedules
and remember to say, "God willing"?
    My living is moment-by-moment.
Do you count blessings?
That I do also
    and find them uncountable!
For whether we plan or are relieved of plans
    whether we set goals or are given one
    whether we remember God cheerfully
       or He catches our attention
       by thrusting His will upon us
He remains in us
    loving, caring
working out patterns to His glory.

Journal

Another night over. Thank God. Nights are too long. Today Hal and I celebrate another wedding anniversary. "You get dressed up, and I will take you out to dinner," he told me last night. We just smiled at each other, knowing it is impossible.

November 5

Hospital.
"Behold, I go now to Jerusalem
bound in the Spirit
    not knowing what shall befall me
except that the Spirit
testifies to me
    that afflictions await me." (Acts 20:22, 23)

Tests.
New doctors, nurses, routines.
Far. Far from home.
Remembrances crowd around my bedside
    loneliness crouches in the corner.
"Does it seem good to Thee to oppress?" (Job 10:3)

Pain
    fear
        more pain
comfort from the nurses
but
clinging to God
    is more comfort than all.

"My own clothes abhor me" (Job 9:31)
but God does not
"for He has not despised or abhorred
    the affliction of the afflicted,"
even cancer

"and He has not hid His face from her,
    but has heard, when she cried to Him." (Ps. 22:24)

November 6

The pain was so great that sweat ran down my back. My hands clenched the X-ray table. I shut my eyes. The barium enema, I was discovering through that great teacher Experience, is not exactly fun.

"Mrs. Hoffman," someone said into my darkness, "this is your doctor." "Hello," I gritted. "What seems to be your main trouble?" he asked foolishly. "*Enemas*," I said. "Before this?" His voice held the trace of a smile. "All the *other* enemas," I answered. I just wanted him off my back.

"How do you feel now?" he persisted. How did he think I felt? "Groovy," I answered. "Groovy," he repeated, unclenching my hands from the X-ray plates.

I was moved into a different position, and I screamed. Pain is extremely personal. "If we do this quickly, we'll get done sooner," he soothed. "Do your thing, Doc," I said through clenched teeth. "But I reserve the right to cry. It's *my body*." He just smiled. He knows.

SEE, SEE!

I was afraid of death.
See, see what God has done!
Now if I am healed
    (or not)
I can counsel those who are dying.
I can say
    I have been there
    where you are
standing at death's door
helpless and trembling
    and God came
    and I tremble no more.
His hand held mine
His victory became all I need.
I can say
Don't be afraid. Walk right on through.
God has been there before you
    and I shall be along
        presently.

Journal
1972
November 8

I have lost 20 pounds in a little over 2 weeks. Bad sign. But I will look good for the casket. (Why do I always make jokes? It isn't funny.) Remember to trust God's mercy.

I sleep no more than 3½ hours a night, for many weeks now. Another reversal. But the nights are usually peaceful, prayer-filled. I thank God utterly for them.

November 9

"What's the verdict, Doc? What's the diagnosis, the prognosis? Can you tell me anything?" He just patted my arm and walked out. I guess he is not ready to say.

But I have been given literature to read: "The cancer victim . . ."

Nov. 9, 1972
"Abed" as they say

Dear Paul,

I'm here for tests and therapy. I received the cassette tape. Thank you! The first hearing, at midnight, brought many tears and good cleansing. I'll listen again today during my IV therapy. (Did you know there are 26,110 drops in an IV?)

I've flunked 12 13 tests, squeaked by on a couple, and sailed through several. (E. g., I don't *also* have diabetes. I have hypoglycemia!)

The dr. hints (or am I exaggerating hope?) that he holds for a lengthier prognosis. Shall I raise my hopes? No. I am an observer, a reporter to the goings-on of my body. The contraindications are new patches found on the colon.

Amy tucks me in for the night and pats my hand. "Gonna be a'right, Mommy, gonna be *a'right!*"

Amen, Lord Jesus!
Dona

Journal

I am a coward. It is wrong to want to die — at least for the reasons I now present. But is it living to watch others do your share of the work? Is it living to hear young voices and not be able to help instruct them, to share their doubts and faith? Is it living to NOT serve? I ache, heart and soul, to serve others. How many more winters and springs shall I see? It shouldn't matter, but today it does. God forgive. God help. Another shudder passes through me. Self-pity is a sin.

November 12

In Seattle we knew that my liver and pancreas were not working. Now my thyroid joins them. A friend asked, "What else can go wrong?" And I said, "Stop asking that question!"

Remembering the first supper tray in the hospital: It looked like there was soy sauce on it, a little pitcher of soy sauce. My tray also carried a bowl of green jello (insult to any hospital patient), a bowl of chicken broth, and a napkin. Oh, yes, a straw (for the soup?) and a half-glass of water which used to be ice, now just mush.

Anyway, it looked like soy sauce, smelled like soy sauce, and the soup could stand some improving, so I poured it in. At that moment I realized it was a pitcher of strong cold tea, with which to make iced tea, using the mushy ice water in the glass. Makes lousy soup. I gave it to Fred, the fly.

Fred landed head-down, fanny-up in the Jello. Gave him that, too. I was not hungry.

The nurse came in and killed Fred with a "fly flap." Poor Fred. He was a good friend.

November 14

Pastor Bob traveled over a hundred miles one way to visit me in the hospital. I just didn't believe it. He smiled, "Well, I wanted to test my new car," but I know him better than that.

November 15

One of the tests at the hospital showed degeneration of the "thoracic spine," which I didn't even know existed. The thorax: Isn't that the second bump on an *ant?* . . .

When I got home from the hospital, there was a gigantic sign across the two townhouses, "Welcome home, Mom." Someone poured balloons from an upstairs window, and everyone sang, "For she's a jolly good fellow," except those of us who were crying, which was nearly all. Tami had baked me a cake.

They were very quiet when they saw my cane. Big Mike cried, after I'd been home awhile. I felt very helpless before such love, such open misery.

Early this morning, Amy had a nightmare. I was downstairs writing when I heard her cry. By the time I got upstairs, she was sitting in bed, partly awake. I held her.

How many nightmares ahead? God — surround my children!

HOME, DEFINED

Who would have thought
that I could call this place home?
But now—
    the old furniture
    the familiar smells
    the neighbor-sounds
all waiting for me, symbolic of heaven—
now I understand:
    home is any corner
    where Love has made a place for you.

Mobile, Ala.
Nov. 27, 1972

Dear Paul,

I sure cry a lot. Sometimes I have to stop everything. . . .

> Like lightning streaking through the dark sky
> the thought *God loves even me*
> streaks through me
>> devastating
>> magnificent
> and I must stop where I am
> to reflect upon the wonder of it!

At night I sleep very little. Maybe 3 hours. Very early
Sunday morning I was reading through some prayers when
I came upon "Scatter the counsels." Your name came to
mind immediately. Then I found the addendum, which
I wrote when we were being sued for something that wasn't
true: "Have compassion, O Lord, upon those who are so
lonely they must turn to evil for solace, and so prideful that
they have blinded themselves to Truth. Open them to love
and to freedom."

I was in the hospital for 1 week. I am going back for
another week on Dec. 3. More tests and therapy. I was
supposed to be there 3 weeks, initially, but I said I'd rather
come back. I am a coward because of the pain. I'm allergic to
all "caines," all barbiturates. I do not take anything stronger
than buffered aspirin with prayer. Therefore, Doc, a week at
a time is enough.

Everyone had turkey for Thanksgiving. I had nausea,
which isn't *any*thing like turkey. But it was a blessed
weekend. The kids have already finished the annual

41

Christmas window. (I was voted down when I suggested a mistletoe design. We have the Baby and the Star. A rare psychological move on my part.) I feel strangely good today — like I will live forever.

Thank you for sharing yourself with me. I love you. Agape of course.
Dona

TELL ME HOW

My courage is facade
countless lashings
    have not aligned my will to God's
    nor cleansed my soul from guilt.
I still lie here
    jealous
    angry
    ashamed of how my hopes are built
aghast at my limp thanks
my songs all torn
    and the way my paper faith has worn.
"Trust in God" — O fellow traveler, tell me
how?
    how can I —
    till this deep shudder passes by.

Journal

1972
December 7

I stumbled and hit my head against the wall.
(I am back in the hospital.) "I don't want to die like
this!" I cried out to the empty room. "How *do* you
want to die, Dona?" a calm voice asked. I turned
around. Pastor Bob was sitting in the big chair.
"Neat. I want to die *neat*," I said. We both smiled,
and he was gone.

I know I imagined him there—yet panic was no
longer in charge of me, so I took it as a comfort
from God.

To PASTOR BOB

The hours are yearlong after you leave.
Precious your visit, and now
time is again stretched taut
    across this hospital room.
Yet I thank God for memory:
    the way our conversations
    and the sweet gift of your presence
    abide here.

Journal

1972
December 8

Friends wrote, saying, No, they weren't praying for mercy, they were expecting healing, and *that only* was their prayer. Despite my request for pure love and mercy, which may be bodily healing and may not. . . .

I have been very disturbed about it. If health is God's only will, why was Paul afflicted? If life, why was young John beheaded? And why does the Psalmist say, "Precious is death"? How dare the book of Deuteronomy pronounce God's awfulness, "I kill and I make alive," unless death to God is the same as life? It is all one to the Christian. How can one state be more desirable than the other — except, as St. Paul explains it in 2 Cor. 4, we prefer "death" because then we are with the Lord.

These friends have prevented my sharing anything more than a how-are-you-I-am-fine. I thank God for Harold, and for Paul, and Pastor Bob, and a few others who are not adverse to sharing anguish and pain and silence from God.

CRY FOR RELEASE

Let me be a voice for the dying:
Lord, deliver me from the healers!
You have not touched my depths —
    scorn not my heights!
What hell is mine by your sweet patience
set against my misery,
    your holy power
    against the stronghold of my welcome Flight.
Oh lay your hands upon the faithless: the gods
absconded with their hope
    whose god is Now
    and death is fear — fear of Night.
Yes — give them day
(if day is truly what they grieve)
    but spare me from your healings
    your touch, which cannot know
the stars come out, the velvet peace steal through,
the untold Love where souls do not remember pain
    and music greets each splendid hour of Night.

47

Dear Dona,

Are you back home? What was it Darius said after that awful night? "Dona, servant of the living God, has your God, whom you serve continually, been able to deliver you from the lions?" How hard it must have been for him to dare to ask that—and then wait in suspense for an answer! Yet how simple it was for him—at least he understood about lions.

My sister Ruth was hospitalized 3 weeks at the end of November—walking pneumonia followed by pleuresy and pericarditis. It will be a long and slow recovery. From a previous hospitalization she knows about IVs. So I made up our "card" for her, with Ruth in place of Dona, and told her something about you. Now I want to make a Xerox of our correspondence and send it to her. She will love you as I do (agape, of course,) a very kindred spirit. Maybe I'll send her your tape, too, your voice with its beautiful capacity for dramatic expression. (Do you sing too? How come God has given you so many talents?) We had an older sister, Thea, who died suddenly of a brain aneurysm 6 years ago, age 46.

Winter has come early, much snow already. Nine below zero yesterday, icy rain this morning. Do I guess right from your poems that you came from North Dakota originally? I get little scraps of biography here and there. What fun it would be to talk to you, if the Lord should choose to open the opportunity, and to know your family, and to talk over with you and Hal the frustrating and forever amateurish art of being parents to teen-agers. I find comfort in Matt. 6:27. If our children cannot add cubits to their stature by worrying about growing, neither can we parents. Is it

escapism to leave so much to the Lord? Pooky tends to think it is, and maybe I'm guilty more than I know. Yet
I sometimes think one of the greatest things God had in mind when He created sexuality is that children should experience two parents, whose thinking is not always the same.

The Lord surround you with Christmas angels, fill you with all joy and peace and hope, and deliver you from every evil, as He has promised!

Much love, in Christ,
Paul

Journal

1972
December 11

Nightmare: Amy is far away, and I am unable to go to her to help. I must watch her cry.

HANG TIGHT

It is a quiet bewilderment
surrounds my soul:
    too many hours alone
    too many nights to think.
Time is hung, head-down
upon the scaffold of Silence.
The Son of Man
    does not always enter the chamber
    of my meditation.

TO MORTY THE SPARROW, WHOM GOD LOVES

Bless you, sparrow! You called me back to God!
  I was wallowing in pity
  when your song came
and immediately upon it, God's voice:
Take no heed for the morrow.
  One day at a time, dear sparrow
  you and I
  one day at a time.

Paul, one of the brethren —
From a sistren. A broken sistren, hewn out of Rock.

I feel good again today, even did two loads of wash. "He breathes new life into me" (Ps. 23:2b). My 6-second litany: Thank You, God, for today; let me not think about tomorrow.

On my last day in the hospital I put it to the doctor straight. I said, "Do you realize I take 46 pills every day?" "Yes," he answered. "Well, I have a serious question to ask, Doc," I said. He waited patiently. "I want to know if you do transplants." He was very quiet. "What did you have in mind?" he hedged. "With 46 pills a day, Doc, I need a gizzard," I said. He left the room smiling.

I failed a few more tests, but none that raised the doctor's eyebrow, so I guess they weren't important. (So I don't have a pulse. . . .) It is a different way to vacation: clean bed every day; being attached to your bottle; having shots that assure you you are lying on a couple of porcupines; happy nurses watching you lying there; meals that were surely exhumed; just male nurses when you need the bedpan; call-light on the floor when you are hooked up to IV (otherwise that light is a lump wherever you turn); trying to peel a soft-boiled egg with one hand — not knowing it is soft-boiled, of course; waiting for the doctor's 1-minute visit with ludicrous intensity; having a whirlpool bath and emerging with a kind of swampy glamor; dropping the fig-leaf towel into the water; being attended by a nurse whose face and demeanor are as animated as a dead flounder, whose countenance would make a good frontispiece for the book of Lamentations.

From the Journal:
Doctor: How do you feel? Me: Groovy. He: Which
groove? Me: Any one. He leans over so nurse doesn't
hear. "You're wonderful," he says. I cry. He probably
tells that to all his rich, good-looking, brave, funny
patients. I am NOT wonderful. But I don't tell him that.

Aside from the malignancy, tests show that I have spinal
degeneration, tachycardia, mercury and lead poisoning,
hypoglycemia, and other un- and re- lated problems. Like
I said once, my body is a 3-credit course at the U.

The poisoning has affected my coordination, so I use
a cane, which I have titled "The Lord," after your sermons
on Eph. 5:15, "Walking Wisely," and Prov. 3:5, "Leaning
on the Lord." We are fairly sure that the damage is
temporary, and it will be good, someday, not to have to
crawl up the stairs or go up one-and-one. Those are my
present choices. (A multiple-sclerosis victim in the next
room said, "But you *have a choice:*" oh.)

Love and great joy through Him who overcame Caesar
Disgustis and the world,

Dona

Dec. 19, 1972

Dear Hal and Dona,
   Sara, Mike, Larry, Dan, Tami, and Amy,

   One of the joys of writing to Dona is that I get to know
you all a little through her. I really wish there were a way
to visit you.

   Thank you, Harold, for sharing your wife with me a little
through her letters, and you, children, for sharing your
mother. She has given me a great deal, not only poems and
writings, but a chance to know her, one other saint in God's
kingdom. It is so rare a privilege to really know another
person. God so wants it to happen in marriage — sometimes
it doesn't happen even there. And if it really happens in
other relationships, it is a rare gift and enrichment indeed!
I think maybe that for all her wisdom and gifts, she is the
littlest child in your household. It is God's own doing, of
course, through the Spirit. But that makes and keeps her
truly beautiful, and lovely.

   I know you won't let her get cocky through my saying
this. You know her faults too well (she *must* have some), and
you add to them your own.

                              Much love in Christ our Lord,
                              Paul

early in the morning
Dec. 24, 1972

Paul—

Well! Like wow! Prisca called me. By now you know you
and Pooky [Paul's wife] are coming here for a few days
(barring complications). And my first thought is, "That
Christmas present is not for Paul, but for me," and my
second is, "They will be disappointed." But Harold says
no—"Even if they are disappointed in us, they're intelligent
enough to use the time as a welcome distraction from a busy
schedule."

"She must have some faults"—that really brought
laughter. I said, "But you know I don't." "Yes, mother,"
they chanted obediently, disbelieving.

I am on a "high." Perhaps it is your approaching visit.
Maybe it is the many Christmas cards and letters I received,
with the miss-yous (and I didn't know they even knew I was
present some Sundays), the thank-yous, and the prayers for
recovery. It is quite possible my high is a simple case of
ego-edema. Whatever, don't analyze it. I like it.

See y'all* January 3 at 2:06 p. m.!
Dona

* We talk like that down south.

55

Dec. 27, 1972

Dear Dona,

Writing to you has always been almost as much of a joy
for me as hearing from you. This time it is hard. Ever since
Prisca's imagination and heart dropped that little bomb
on us Christmas Eve — plane tickets to your city — I have
been trying to figure out some way to come and visit you.
But there are just too many complications. It is hard not
to come, harder still to tell that to Prisca, and to you. Yet
maybe there would have been great complications at your
end, too. I lean much on Rom. 8:28, that in spite of griefs
of the moment the Lord works everything for good for us,
if we can just hang in there a little longer and love and
trust Him. Maybe He intends it some other time, some other
way. Can you forgive me?

Thanks for your detailed report on your hospital
experience and the complexity of diagnoses. No doubt
questions like, "Where did you get such things as lead and

mercury poisoning?" are quite useless at this point. I noticed the cane on your graffiti and wondered. Dona, Dona, how I pray for you — for your continued courage, for your hope, for your deliverance from pain, for your healing!

I wanted to read Pastor Jay your sentence about a nurse "whose countenance would make a good frontispiece for the book of Lamentations," then decided to read him the whole paragraph. We found ourselves splitting with laughter — porcupines, exhumed meals, swampy glamor. By the time we got to that last sentence, I had to hand him the letter and let him read it himself. And yet there is such pain in the humor. Is that why God makes humor possible? As love covers a multitude of sins, so laughter covers pain.

Thanks for the poems. Keep baking your bread — the sales department is the Lord's business. You have at least one eager customer.

Much love, also to your family,
Paul

1972
December 30, 10:30 p. m.

   Phone call to Paul Bretscher from Harold Hoffman (had tried earlier at 7:30 and 10): Your parish
down here needs you. Please come. Dona is entering
the hospital again Jan. 7. Very painful treatment.

How grateful I am, Paul, that you came! I pray you are not sorry.

You made me feel so good while you were here. No stumbling (well, not a lot), little pain. "You don't look like hospital fodder," you said. Harold laughed when I told him that. "He should know you like I do," he said. I have been well taught to cover how I really feel. So be it. The world needs a laugh now and then. God knows. I'm sorry there is no time to rewrite this. Nurse is here to mail this. I *do* feel better (not this moment but usually).

Dona

Journal

1973
January 11
Hospital

"It's like this, Doc," I said, finally getting his attention. "You want to go, say, from the bed to the hall, and the door is open. But you don't know how to get there. Something blocks your brain from thinking, 'Stand up, put one foot in front of the other, and you're there.' Is this a symptom of anything, Doc?"

"Derangement," he replied, smiling.

Jan. 17, 1973

Dear Dona,

Your "Yes, Lord" is posted in the middle of my office bulletin
board, surrounded by a clutter of reminders of many things,
and right over my typewriter. It is a beautiful piece of art.
It is also a miracle. How can anybody keep saying "Yes,
Lord" when it means to let go something you love and want
very much — or even worse, to walk into darkness, pain,
cross, and death? "Yes, Lord" — it's all there in that picture,
the whole Christian faith and life, the dark cross and the
colors that depict promises of beauty that see us through.
But then it gets so dark that even those colors fade, till only
the white "Yes, Lord" remains. How can it, when you don't
see a thing? It's a miracle. You must hate to say it, dread
to say it, fight and cry against it — and yet in the end you
keep coming back to it. That's the Lord's miracle of beauty

in you, and only in that does all your natural created beauty make enduring sense forever and ever and ever. For that can't be you; it's got to be Christ and His Spirit dwelling in you.

As for "distractions," you are still my favorite. As Eccl. 3 has it, "There is a time to be distracted and a time to resist distraction." I'm sure the Lord wants me to be distracted by Dona. Think of all the times He was distracted! What better thing could He have done with those moments in which He blessed the little ones or answered the cry of the Canaanite mother or let a woman anoint Him?

If Jesus was enriched with joy by His distractions, He must not mind that I am enriched too!

God keep you in His love and peace, and your family too,
Paul

Jan. 21, 1973

Dear Paul,

Thank you for your beautiful letter. You are so right
about the "Yes, Lord." I fight and cry against it. Now I am
suspended between the hope of living and the hope of
dying, and I must say it yet again.

I wonder if you have ever encountered anyone who
was not sure he could face the pain of getting well only to
die again another day. Perhaps the problem is academic:
I have no choice.

Thank you for letting me be your distraction. I think
you have very loosely translated "time to kill" to mean
distraction! I only know I am grateful for every moment
you can spare for me — whether in print or in person. You
make me feel useful, even when I most definitely am not.

At last someone wants my bread! (I should maybe cut
down on production.)

In Christian love,
Dona

SUBMISSION

Oh God the pain
Is there no way
    I can offer this
    as sacrifice?
Your grace covers me
Your love warms me
    but if it hurt
    one iota more
    I could not bear it.
How carefully
You measure out strength
against pain!
    In all Your wealth
    could You not give
    an extra ounce
so that I might rise
    above it

Or does it please You
  that I am helpless
  and come crying to You
        moment upon moment?
  So be it. Dear God
  I love You anyway.

Journal

1973
January 28

    It would be better if there were no good days.
The good days only serve to emphasize the bad days.
How I empathize with those who serve by waiting!
        Will You heal me, Lord?
        And when I awoke
        there was blood on the fleece
           and signs of great struggle.

TOUCH

A nurse touched the dying boy
and he cried.

> Did I hurt you? she asked.

> No, he said, you touched me.

>> No one has touched me since I came here.

Touch the dying
> for where they go
> I go

>> and where I go
>> you follow.

Dear Paul,

Your sister Ruth wrote a beautiful letter thanking me for the 77(!) pages of correspondence between us. I must either quit writing so much or find another listener!

Your New Year's Eve offering [of a tape] reminds me of the grasshopper part of me, and the giants in the land of my fears. Do you know these giants? Like getting well. It seems possible that I will. But it is a long way to come back, after having been so far down the road; and knowing I must return again another day does not help. I wonder if you can understand that. If I should be overcome with gratitude, understand that I am not. I am still very tired and wonder if the journey back is worth it.

Being touched satisfies a desire to be needed as a physical presence. You cannot know until no one touches you, how you miss the physical contact of others. "God has not shrunk in loathing from the plight of the downtrodden" (Ps. 22:24). Thank You, God.

Amy has to see the doctor again today. She has her very own Resident Cough Germ. She has missed so much school, she may have to repeat first grade. "Am I very sick?" she asked. "I don't know," I replied. We were sitting in the big rocker. I read to her from Psalm 56: "When I am afraid, I put my trust in Thee," and we prayed together.

We are both afraid—of pain, of loneliness, of not knowing, of growing. It is comforting to hear David say "when," not "if." But I am confronted with a giant of such size that I have not ceased to tremble.

Dona

Journal

Hilarious: My horoscope reads, "Prepare for new elegance in your circle." I don't even *have* a circle!

My energy level is higher, but I have more pain. What shall I make of it? There is nothing to do except go on, one day at a time. It is so frustrating, having a *mind* enclosed in a body which refuses to function right.

Feb. 9, 1973, 2:30 a. m.

Dear Paul,

This past week: hell. Hours of hell. No tears. The pain
was beyond tears. Now the lessening again, and I wonder if
it was all just a nightmare. Other signs, too, indicate all is
not as well as I thought, and I am back on a diet of fresh
vegetables, fruits, juices. ("How about worms, Doc?"
"They're okay if you really *dig worms*.") I still firmly
believe I will get well, but not on my terms.

Tami was awake in her room (across from mine) during
the worst night. She crept downstairs to Harold and asked,
"Couldn't you buy Mommy some pretty flowers? She hurts
so much." "But it's dark, honey," he said; "the stores aren't
open." "Tomorrow then," she insisted. The next morning:
"Are you better, Mommy?" "I am better," I said. "Oh!"
A beautiful smile. It was all the bouquet anyone could want.

> To wrest from every savage moment
> the infinite peace of God
> to cling to His promises
> even when my heart would be a scoffer
> to live abundantly and with joy
> centering my thoughts upon Him
> this is the challenge
> the goal
> and the prize.

Dona

70

Journal

1973
February 14

Much pain lately.

Feb. 28, 1973

Dear Dona,

Let me take a little recess from sermon work — things aren't breaking through anyhow at the moment — to write to you. I think maybe I've restrained the impulse long enough. Besides, it's a great text, the Epistle for this Sexagesima Sunday, 2 Cor. 11:16 — 12:9. Longest in the book — the boasting in weakness and shame and suffering, in prayers unanswered, in visions which weren't really yours after all — so that his people will stop looking at him and at the glory-preachers who attract so much attention to themselves, and look at nothing but the grace of God, the power of Christ. What looks so empty, so foolish — promises, a cross — is so full! "For the sake of Christ I am content with weakness, for when I am weak, then I am strong." "My grace is sufficient!"

We never finish learning it, but you have learned it enough to celebrate it, teach it, hang onto it in your hardest moments. That's no credit to you — it's kind of like being somebody else, the way Paul talks of being somebody else in 12:4-5 (or Gal. 2:20, "No longer I, but Christ"). And yet it is you, Dona, the strange halo you wear which invites anyone who sees it to celebrate the grace of God (as in 1 Cor. 15:10). God's true Dona.

Thanks for honoring me by telling me of the pain, the "hours of hell," as well as of the little signals of bouquet, Tami's "beautiful smile." That makes it possible for me to weep as well as rejoice with you. And to say Amen to your striking last last sentence. For it is not just beautifully formulated words. The "savage moment" and the "scoffer" heart are real — but so is the peace of God and His promises.

72

"Whenever our hearts condemn us, God is greater than our hearts, and He knows everything!" (1 John 3:20) *Amen.*

Through it all I think of you much, and your family — wondering whether the moments of suffering are easing or becoming fewer, how the cane labeled "The Lord" is doing, how Pastor Bob and Janice are too, how Harold's job is working out for him, when you will take the plunge to buy a house, how Sara's plans are coming, how the rest of the children are doing, and the like. But I know the Lord is holding you as always in His grace and peace.

Heavenly Father, bless and keep Dona on her birthday and always. Let the beauty of Jesus continue to shine through her — for her own simple joy, for her family, for all whose lives are touched by hers! Amen.

Happy Birthday!

Love,
Paul

Journal

1973
March 1

I wake up a dozen times every night, look at the clock, and always discover it is still yesterday. "O Hal," I say to no one in particular, and finally decide to get up. I am freezing cold, not only because the outside temperature registers 30, but also because Hal's Great Nighttime Motto is "One good turn gets the whole blanket," which he probably borrowed from somewhere.

"You getting up?" he asks, *as I am dressing.* "Yes," I say, trying to sound sane. "When you coming back?" he mumbles. I feel a fit of cowardice coming on, because if I tell him, "Never," he will be wide awake in a fifth of a second. If I say, "Later," he will agonize it over and over in his mind and finally come downstairs to *chat* with me, his brain still in limbo. If I say, "When I get warm," he will offer to turn up the heater, and I still won't have a blanket. "I'll be back in a minute or two," I lie. "Mffrp," he replies intelligently.

I come downstairs laden with guilt, looking for a painless way to turn my heart back into stone. I suck my fingers and twirl my hair. "Most people are attached to their navels," I say aloud in a moment of pure revelation.

The horoscope page in the newspaper lies open. I read my future. "Best day in a decade for romantic achievements," it says. Well, now, that's better. This day is going to prove interesting. Especially since I don't know a romantic soul within four galaxies. Check the date. February 28. That was yesterday.

Yesterday — what happened then? *Romance?* Ohhhh yeah. I talked to a handsome human male for a few minutes. Even loaned him a Band-Aid because he had skinned his knee on his kiddie car.

Reduced to a state of functional disintegration, I dial Pastor to tell him I am willing to give up Harold for Lent, then realize it is only 2:30 in the morning. I hang up just as I hear a sleepy "hello." Hopefully, I dialed the wrong number.

Thus ends another episode in the life of Dona Hoffman, Super Christian, who discovers that there's a difference between proclaiming the love of God and living it, between "Let there be light," and finding a match, between "Judas hanged himself," and "Go thou and do likewise."

March 13, 1973

Dear Paul,

I remember your sitting on the couch beside me, saying, "Ask for healing, Dona. He will hear."

I guess I never told you: I had asked for healing, the whole year before I knew I had cancer. I spent hours (no less than 20 minutes a day, every single day; no merit on my part: I'm just telling you) in meditation: "Thank you for healing me, Lord" (this based on Matt. 21:22, "Pray believing"). I yielded myself to Christ, asking Him to pour Himself into every corner of me, healing me. I kept getting worse. I asked then for the prayers of my friends and a Christian healing group. The tests came back worse every time I went to the doctor.

I began to hear myself saying things like, "It isn't working. Prayer is just empty talk." It was when I accepted my illness as the will of God that I could talk to Him eye-to-eye once more.

"Work out whatever plan You may have for my body, Lord. I know that my soul is safe with You." That was the Corner Prayer (taking another direction). Whatever others may be allowed to ask, I know that I am to request no miracles.

Health report: I am about back to the point that I was when I first entered the hospital last November. Except for the pain. More than November, less than January and February, it has decreased in opportunity if not intensity.

My mind doesn't blank out as much as it used to. I walk up the stairs more often. "The Lord" still supports me on any journey longer than the length of this apartment. My digestive tract watches over my diet to keep me honest. Tachycardia continues to keep my heart occupied, especially at night.

In Christ,
Dona

Journal

1973
March 19

I am better. Pain still takes hold of me and has its victories. And nausea has prevented my being able to eat, many times. But enough good hours come that I am able to prepare my lessons on Philippians. How I love God! I am not always able to feel His returning love, but I know it is there, just as I know the sun is there, even when it is not shining.

March 31, 1973

Dear Dona,

Harold called Thursday night with news your pain is so great you have to enter the hospital for another week of treatment. I'm so sorry, Dona! I live in the illusion that the pain and periods of pain must surely be subsiding a little. I delight that you are able to undertake a Bible class. And then —

"Remember Dona in mercy, Lord, with rest and healing of body as well as with courage of Spirit to trust you still!"

You promised, Lord, "My presence will go with you, and I will give you rest." You fulfilled it so wonderfully in Jesus! And now, Lord, for His sake, be present with Dona! Hold her close. Don't leave her alone. And give her REST! Amen. (Ex. 33:14)

Much love and peace, in Christ,
Paul

April 1-2-3-4-5? Choose one.

Dear Paul,

It's early Wednesday, I guess. My eyes are nearly back in focus, and I have read your letter. Hal says, too, that you prayed for me after the accident in drugs. Thank you.

Does anything ever happen by accident? What lesson was to be learned by whom, and I the practice board?

Being here is like giving birth to a stillborn. Pain, but no welcome cry. Just pain, bombarding the walls of my faith. But "faith should have no walls"!

And nightmares. Mass hysteria of all the beings that people my dreams. Nocturnal anxieties enough to keep Poe lucrative another 50 years. Keep joking, Dona, it's nearly daybreak.

I know why. Last winter I gave myself over to God. Now I am fighting with Him. I am well enough to want to work, not well enough to do anything. Yuk.

Yet I love God and recognize His mercy—that unmerited love for me. Like warring lovers, she adamantly wrong, He gently and persistently right, God and I continue to battle for dominance.

Guess what—IV Roto-Rooter time.

Dona

XYLOCAINE

Clever of You, God.
I have to smile at You.
I come for the next lesson
    just a little bit smug, don't I
    having learned the last so well.
But You make sure
by vomit and pain and blood and helplessness
that I am stripped of dignity
    properly conditioned to learn.
You withdraw a gift or ten
    to keep my lessons on humility
    fresh and meaningful.

Journal

1973
April 10

Prescriptions for this month, only $188. I'm back on 33 pills a day, which is better than 46, my previous high.

Hal just shrugs his shoulders at the bill (we had to pay cash for the drugs, which is sometimes quite difficult), and says, "Oh, well, another income tax deduction."

Just two more visits and I'll have their new wing paid for. This last time I had not only the usual infusions to contend with, but they began the week by giving me Xylocaine, to which I am extremely allergic. I was in a semiconscious state for a long while. Vomiting, lying in vomit because I could not call or press the call-light. My eyes still do not focus well.

Tami is lying in the living room with me, hoping to work up a fever. She does have a little cold, but I was hoping the kids could make it through the week so I could recuperate a bit. I guess she's lonesome, and that's when the bones ache more.

April 11, 1973

Dear Dona,

I appreciated Harold's call so much last Wednesday, with the report that you had come through the crisis of the -cain "accident," and that things were getting back to whatever counts as normal for Dona. Your letter arrived on Saturday with more details and with the usual precious reflection of struggle, faith, and courage.

Your reference to the IV Roto-Rooter is funny and intriguing. Does that analogy have some medical validity?

I notice that the text for April 29 (John 21:15-19) contains Peter's "Yes, Lord." Fascinating! This Sunday, the Epistle, Phil. 2:5-11. Can we really think the way Jesus thought? Does the form of God show in the form of the servant? What a strange concept of God, who Himself is concerned not to rule but to serve, who asks Jesus to put on His form and invites us to have that same mind too — emptying ourselves, letting it all go, so that He may fill us! Confess it. Jesus Christ is Lord!

To the glory of God the Father,
Paul

Journal

1973
April 12

Tami brought the pillow and blanket to me as I lay on the floor, doubled up in pain. Then she put her head on my hand. When I could talk, I said, "Did you know, Tami, that I thank God many times that He let you come into my life?" "I thank Him for you too," she said, then added, "usually. But some nights I don't remember to."

"That's all right. He knows," I said. "He sees that there is something special between you and me."

"It *is* special," she said. Then, "Momma, if you die, there won't be anybody around here to care about me." I could feel warm tears on my hand. "You're the only one who cares."

Not true, not true. But under the stress of the moment, very true to Tami.

May 2, 1973

Dear Paul,

   Surgery. Surviving by grit and grace has never been one of my favorite pastimes. Please pray for an extra measure of grace. My surplus of grit has diminished considerably. May 13 is my entrance date for the Grand Opening. I just talked to Doc on the phone.

   How blessed I am that you should come into my life, bringing such abundance!

We are God's children. . . .
Dona

WHEN I CLIMBED MOUNTAINS

You never knew me
    when my eyes were seldom off the sky
    and my hands could paint in oils or fold the
        towels with equal zest
    and visions were expanded until life was lived
        on highs
    of hope and gift and praising God, and rest
        was something others did.
You never knew me
    when I climbed mountains! breathing new ideas
        in and out
    and there upon the tawny cliffs how God infilled
        my emptiness
    and life became a shout,
        a constant stream.
You never knew the kind of dream
that held it all together.
                Fragile world.

You know me now
and I wonder at your knowledge of my depth
    and if you understand the giving-up of self

and hope, and mountaintops
the agony when life runs dry
and I no longer am accorded highs
and every happiness must be dearly bought
from commonness.
Once life was large—with all that that implies—
and you knew me not at all. I
apologize.

May 7, 1973

Dear Dona,

Jubilate! So you go in for surgery, mountaintop to valley,
Mother's Day to hysterectomy. "Make a joyful noise to the
Lord. Rejoice in the Lord always." God's strange humor, but
it is beautiful to laugh at Satan, to defy what we see, to rest
in One crucified, to look away from what would invite
self-pity, and thus to understand your line "This praise—it's
much too large for me!"

Thanks for "When I Climbed Mountains."

I've been studying Matt. 14:22-33. I think it tells of Jesus'
death and resurrection. The waves and darkness of threat
and death come like a flood to drown and swallow him up
(Ps. 42:7, 69:1-2, 15; Jonah 2:3). But Jesus defies the flood,
in all loneliness persists in love, does it God's way. The
darkness and flood don't get Him; He actually walks on the
water! He comes to the disciples in their futility and terror
of those waves and darkness (Easter). They can only think
He is a ghost, but He says, "It is I; don't be afraid." Jesus
is back in the boat with them—and John 6 says that
immediately they are at their destination. The Kingdom is
here; they have eternal peace when they have Him! So we
stand in awe and confess Jesus alone to be the Son of God.
The mockers lied; they are wrong. All who called Him the
blasphemer are wrong. Jesus alone is the Son, and we
through Him.

So now we with Peter say, "Lord, bid me come to You
on the water," and He says, "Come." We too will defy all
the evidences of darkness and death, cling to the promises,
do the Father's will in the face of defeat and disaster.
"Come!" And we come, but so do the temptations, the

89

waves which seem to mock obedience and make walking on the sea ridiculous. So we sink and cry, "Help! Lord, save me!" Immediately His hand is there to catch us. He understands our "little faith," our "doubt," but only to comfort and hold us, not to accuse. You've been walking on the water, Dona! And when you have cried, His hand has always been there and will be. That's the greatest miracle — greater than mountains and sunsets. Frail Dona, full of pain, knowing the terror of waves and darkness — rejoicing in her Lord, wanting to come to Him, responding to His "Come!" — walking on the sea. "Jubilate!" Wow! What hath God wrought?

Strange miracle, though. Nobody does this one to "show off."

Greet Hal, Sara, Dan, Larry, Tami, and Amy — also Mike.

Much love, courage, and hope
in Christ,
Paul

Journal

1973
May 9

Surgery scheduled next week. Not minor, as planned. In purple ink on my tummy I made a sign for Doc: ⟶
Certainly hope he has a sense of humor.

U.S.D.A. CHOICE

May 10

Paul

   I have reached a new low, Paul—and will write later
when I am come up again.

D

I PUT ON THESE SHOES

I put on these shoes
but I do not want to walk
    where You tell me I must go.
I did not hesitate, Lord
when You said
    Put away your slippers
    and take these walking shoes
but the path You point to
is nearly vertical
    and I am afraid.

(I received a card, with the message "Bless the Lord, O my soul, and all that is within me, bless His holy name!" — and this hand-written note on the day I was to have had surgery.)

Monday, 2 p. m., May 14, 1973

Dear Dona,

Perhaps you are in surgery even now. You are much in my heart, and God's — and in my prayers. Your note came this morning, "a new low" you confess — also those shoes facing that steep mountain.

"Show me a token for good" (Ps. 86:17). Show Dona one, Lord. Just a little sign to pick her up out of such depths, something she can see and feel, and so find Your promise and hope in it as a token of Your goodness! Reach out your hand and draw her to You out of the sea. Give her rest and a quiet expectation. Set her table with blessing in the midst of so many enemies. Silence the accuser, clothe her in wedding dress of the saints (Zech. 3:1-4), sustain her through every crushing misery, and relieve her of pain. How long does it have to be, Lord? Oh, satisfy her early with Your mercy! Let the beauty of the Lord, her God, be upon her!

Much love in Christ,
Paul

                          at the hospital
                          May 14, 1973, 10 a. m.

"When I am afraid, I put my trust in Thee."
"Whom have I in heaven beside Thee? There
is nothing upon earth that I desire besides
Thee. My heart and my flesh may fail, but
God is my portion forever!"

Dear Paul,

He came back. I opened the door to my low emotional state, and He came back in. Thank God that He can humble Himself to knock at my door! Oh, truly He is great to make Himself to small! I cannot understand such love. Happiness is letting God be Lord over all thought and desire.

"His greatness is unsearchable!"

I wonder — repeatedly, for the experience is almost monotonous in its continual restatement — why, when it is so fulfilling to be alive in Christ, we resent dying to self. Over and over, in tedious repetition, I must learn this lesson. Is it like this for everyone, or do others, once comprehending, submit utterly and only once? How is it with you?

Today I have given the hospital staff a new thrill: Find something Dona's not allergic to, so she'll be relaxed enough that we can put an oxygen tube down her throat during surgery. A skin test coming up. Some new drug . . .

They're gonna remember me.

It is noon. Lunch (that was lunch?) has come and gone. . . .

tests this morning
more this afternoon
X-rays
vampires draw blood
more "kidney specimens"
but
I
am
not
afraid.

Dona

96

IF YOU MUST

From pedestals and praise
    lift me to humility
from piety and honor
    raise me to pain
from hope in temporal things
    unburden me.
Lift me to despair if You must
so that despairing
    I cry to You
and in pain
    I seek Your grace
and like a little child, find hope
    simply in belonging.

Journal

1973
May 16

No surgery. Doc told Hal I'd have died "on the table" (a gruesome expression) if he'd gone ahead with it. So it was best.

I called Paul long-distance the following morning, and he said, "But can you survive without the surgery?" And I reminded him that I would not have survived *with* it.

Doc will scout around for some new drug. Surgery postponed 30 to 60 days.

May 19, 1973

Dear Paul,

By some stroke of luck it is Saturday afternoon and I am alone in the house! At least for a few minutes.

My doctors haven't let me know of any progress in finding a drug. Hal will call Doc next week. "Poor surgical risk, adverse reaction to anesthetics, susceptible to shock."

It overwhelms me to have you for my friend. Your love speaks to me, comforts me, always Christ-ward.

Love undefinable,
Dona

May 17, 1973

Dear Dona,

What's next for Dona, Lord? Hypnotism? Acupuncture?
Lord, You have a strange way of teasing those You love,
paying attention to them by setting out one crisis after
another. But aren't You getting a little tired of it by now?
Can't You show her Your love another way—cuddle her,
let her rest?

Much love in Christ,
Paul

May 21, 1973, midnight, more or less

Dear Paul,

I cried reading your letter. I want you to know I put it off, not knowing why, opened all my other mail, sat staring at the envelope until I knew I'd better open it or I'd not have time to cry before the kids came home. Somehow I knew I'd cry.

Why do you affect me so? I think it is because in the deep empty places of my soul I find a companion in you. You speak an understanding I have not met before. You sense my agonies and help me carry them a little way. You give no quick answers or do-it-yourself helps. Only that that the Lord calls compassion. (Now you know my tears were not sad. Grateful.)

The mountain was laid low, but not because I had anything to do with it. Thank you for praying for me. . . .

Dona

May 23, Finally figured out why I could not mail this.
I knew that it was unfinished. I have just returned from the
third hell — in the body, not out of it, that I know — feeling
things that cannot be told, which cannot be uttered except
in moaning — where God always tests me on the truth of what
I write. My confession: I do not always believe what I say,
or if I believe it, I cannot always follow through. I cannot
always embrace pain or face things bravely. I rebel with my
whole being. Believe it.

D

Journal

1973
May 28

I celebrated the anniversary of the prognosis in an undesirable way: in bed. I'd planned to make a strawberry shortcake, have cold roast beef, salad, etc. But I couldn't stay out of bed long enough to accomplish any part of the menu. By nightfall I could sit outside awhile, and it was quite peaceful.

May 31

Doc showed me my X-rays. "I'll take a dozen of each pose," I said knowledgeably. I think I am wearing him down: Last time I left the hospital, he said, 'You've got to get well or you won't be able to come back." I still cannot understand that statement. . . .

ANNIVERSARY OF THE PROGNOSIS

I had time to sit outside tonight.
Seldom do. It's some perverted sense of duty
holds me back.
Tonight, though, I listened to the night.
I stayed outside until I felt the velvet sky
come down to cover me
    great indigo
    with a few sparks of starshine
the throbbing of the universe
against the puny sound of man.
I felt the night come down to heal my soul.

SONG FOR A SLEEPLESS NIGHT

Though the Lord give you the bread of
    adversity
and the water of affliction,
yet your Teacher will not hide Himself
    any more,

He's in me, beneath me, around me, above me, and beyond me! (Deut. 33:2; Psalm 91:4; Psalm 34:7; John 14:20)

but your eyes shall see your Teacher
and your ears shall hear a word behind
    you saying,
"This is the way, walk in it,"
when you turn to the right
or when you turn to the left.

"I know, O Lord, that it is not in man who walks to direct his own steps." (Jer. 10:2)

You shall have a song
as in the night when a feast is kept;

like midnight Christmas Eve services, holy, precious, beautiful

and gladness of heart

where gladness is real: inner joy

as when one sets out to the sound of the
flute
to go to the mountain of the Lord.

heady air, abundant water flowing freely, new thoughts, reaffirmed values, freshness, life

How did God *know?*

(Is. 30:20, 21, 29 RSV)

Journal

1973
June 3

Today (Exaudi) is the anniversary of Dan and Larry's confirmation. The girls and I put over a small turkey to celebrate.

Exaudi is one of the most meaningful Sundays in the entire church year. "Waiting" Sunday — or as Pastor Hillmann used to say, "Roll with the Punches" Sunday.

The Introit is so beautiful: "When Thou saidst, Seek; my heart said, Lord, *I seek!*" I'm looking, Lord!

It is new to me every year, how Exaudi (especially) fits me. I wait. I try to roll with the punches. I seek.

from "KNOCK GENTLY"

Terror stalks the night
    beats its wings
    over the beds of my children.
Terror twists itself
    into my wringing hands.
Terror
    pushes the minutes
    into timelessness.

The absolute faith of childhood
looked at me
    and I was humbled
    before it.

Walk beside your child
with a careful joy
    he is a stranger
    in a new land
and you have been chosen
    only as his *guide*
    as his *only* guide.

Oh, Mother, Jesus is *born!*
What'll I *do?*
>Let Him live, child.
>Let Him *live.*

Life is not easier Your way, Lord
>but it *is* larger.

There's God —
>looking at me through
>cross-colored glasses.

To wrest from every savage moment
the infinite peace of God
>to cling to His promises
>even when my heart would be a scoffer
to live abundantly and with joy
centering my thoughts upon Him
>this is the challenge
>>the goal
>>>and the prize.

How humble the great sea
>that she should wash
>*my* feet!

June 7, 1973

Dona, dear Dona,

Thank you for your letters and poem, for the riches of
your understanding, for the glowing tidbits of truth and
insight. You have so delightful a gift, to be able to see
things nobody would notice, to catch God's surprises. "How
humble the great sea, that she should wash my feet." What
a gem that is, among so many others in your "Knock gently."
Or your reflection on "One generation shall praise Thy
works to another." Or the way Is. 30 captures you—a
marvelous word, which has seen me through depressions,
too, the Word from behind that says, "This is the way; walk
in it," when you just cannot see where He is taking you.

Did you notice verse 26, the sevenfold light "in the day
when the LORD binds up the hurt of Dona and heals the
wounds inflicted by His blow"? There it is again—He, the
Lord, does the wounding, too! That's the great comfort—
the call to give up our wisdom of "knowing good and evil"
and to walk by the ear of faith rather than by sight. You
capture it in "If You Must." "From pedestals and praise lift
me to humility." That's the wisdom of "the world
upside-down." How I have loved you and God in you, from
the first time I was ever struck to the heart by a poem
of yours!

Thanks for sharing your pain and the "confession" that
goes with it. I know. Do you know how I know? By one of
the greatest discoveries with which God has blessed me—
years of wrestling—what the temptation story of Jesus
really means. He had the Word of God, naming Him "my
beloved Son" (ever human, as in Ex. 4:22-23), promising
Him the inheritance and kingdom, calling Him to

servanthood. But in the temptations all the evidences
conspired against that Word. The Word was empty,
hollow, nonsense. To believe it was fanaticism. And Jesus
survives by sheer stubbornness, against even the accusation
that He can't really believe that any more! I wonder whether
in His conflict there was also a dash of Peter's insight in a
very low moment—"Lord, to whom would we go?" The
alternatives are more hollow still! Who can understand the
Spirit and faith? Let God worry about that. You just listen
still for that Word behind you that says, "This is the way,
Dona; walk in it," even through "loud cries and tears."
(Heb. 5:7)

So now, little rebel Dona, who "cannot always embrace
pain or face things bravely," be a rebel, boldly! The Lord
loves you when you protest, when you fight Him, for in your
very struggle you are seeking Him. I'll join you! "Lord,
where is Thy steadfast love of old, which by Thy faithfulness
Thou didst swear to Dona?" "Lord, you called Dona the
sheep of Your pasture! Why do you slay her all the day long
and count her as a sheep to be slaughtered?" (Ps. 89:49;
44:20-22) *Kyrie eleison!*

But He said, "My grace is sufficient for you." And He did
not spare His own Son.

Joy, peace, and much love,
Paul

June 18, 1973

Dear Paul,

Many times over I have read your warm, absorbing letter.
You took the time to read my "Knock Gently." How do you
know how poets need to be heard? Not necessarily
published, though that is nice, but listened to. It is only
a human need, but much exaggerated in the poet.

Thursday finds me in the big city for more testing. Dear
God, it is an interminable Terminal. (But I hear Paul say,
"He knows, Dona. He knows.") And now another doctor,
a good friend from Seattle, when told the details, said it
does not look too good. But just to keep us guessing: I have
had less pain and just a little more sleep in the past week.
I will let you know about surgery, so that I might tempt
back your prayers on my behalf.

. . . and He cares for me through *you.*
Dona

Journal

1973
June 18

Some days I reach the plane where tears would be a luxury, where pain is the only direction, and the reward for living on is sweat and moaning. It is the bowels of hell.

But my thoughts do not always turn inward. Sometimes I can look upon the face of all suffering — multiplied by infinite time and countless victims — the thousand upon thousand dreams gone to vapor, the hopes stripped and broken — and I know then that my life, my promise, my little dreams gone unheeded are nothing. The larger crime is against those who have not anyone even to care.

God does not lessen our burdens. He only assures us that He cares, and when we finally understand that, nothing else matters.

FUGITIVE

O God don't let it end so soon!
Why
    why must it all be taken back?
No creature has more deeply praised You
    for the gift of a single day's strength
yet
even in its transcience
I recognize the symbol of my own being.

I close myself about the thought of You:
Your mercy is not shadow
    Your grace is not smoke to billow away.
Surely Your love will outlive
all the passing moment of me.

Hello again —

I must have counted very much on having surgery and getting all better. I must have made some sort of god out of my hope. My dream:

A wall. I could not get over it or through it or around it. I kicked at it and pounded my fist against it. I threw my whole body at it, but it would not move. Many people were watching, and I had the feeling that if I could do the right thing *they* would be helped as well as I — but I was unable to discover what that right action might be, and I groped at the wall in blind and utter frustration.

No surgery. "It would be murder." "Professional suicide for any doctor who performed it." "Go home." "People have survived several years with your condition." (But survival, Doc, is not living. Silence.) "Your body certainly deserves surgery." "I'm sorry."

"Where will you go now, Dona? Mayo?" Pastor Bob was here over 2 hours to help me over the hump. "No. I have nowhere else to go for help," I told him. "Just to God. I have to find Him again."

> "When Thou saidst, Seek;
> my heart said, Lord, *I seek.*"
> Dona

THREE VISITORS

Is heaven real?

I cannot answer. I don't know.

Tell me that heaven is real.

I understand how much you need to hear it,

but I can only tell you about today.

Today is real.

Heaven is real. Oh, tell me!

Heaven is real

and God is.

Reality is not in pain or time

but in God. Touch Him.

June 29, 1973

Dear Dona—

No surgery possible. One more little "hope" canceled. "Yes, Lord." It's all right, as long as the one who girds you and carries you where you do not wish to go is the Lord, whom you love.

Much love in Christ,
Paul

Journal

1973
June 30

"God does not remember our sins," Billy Graham says in a telecast. Larry, Dan, and I are watching together. Larry said, "Wow—like you might say, 'I'm sure sorry I did that, God. Can't get it out of my mind,' and God says, 'Get WHAT out of your mind?'"

LAST TIMES

Don't talk to me just now.
I've run the length and breadth of hope—
    the wind will never be so cool again
    the world so large
    nor my raw heart so pained by human voice.
This
is a last time:
    this day will never be again
    and tomorrow may not come.
I flee the wild dark clouds approaching—
I run!
tomorrow may not come!
    oh it is not enough to run!
This child I call my soul has lost its sight
and time is now surrounded by the night
    tomorrow—can you feel it?
    oh tomorrow may not come.

Oh, Paul,

A week of nothing but lying down (smoldering). Then sudden freedom from pain Sunday morning (how good the world seemed!) and only a little discomfort Sunday afternoon. Today (it is noon, Monday) I still feel fairly good, though I can tell I have to slow down again. (Help me not to resent that, Lord.)

It was so good of you and Prisca and Debbie to come to Mobile. I understand the sacrifice and am overwhelmed by the love that shines out of all of you. I wish I had been more "coherent," but I know you understand even that and my stumbling fingers on the piano and the many things left unsaid.

When you are near, God is.
Dona

THAW

Love me with a joyous bounce
    oh do not let love die!
let love laugh or bleed or hope
drink deep of love's intriguing
      but when my love would make you cry
      turn from it, disbelieving.
Let love be fresh and full and happy
    love be dark, with scent of storm
love my winter and my song
but love with joy! oh love me warm!

July 31, 1973

Hello again—

I finally found my baptism certificate in some papers
my mother gave me just before we left Seattle. For the first
time in 41 years I celebrated my baptism birthday. July 24.
Celebrated: No one was there. Just me and God and a
birthday candle stuck into a chocolate cookie. Amy wandered
in, saw a celebration in progress, found Larry. Daniel
happened by. So there were five of us. We cut the cookie
into tiny, pie-shaped pieces and sang "Happy Baptism."

You have more to do than read my long letters. But I am
so very grateful that you do read them!

God surround you, fill you,
support you.
Dona

Dear Paul,

I've read the 77 pages of correspondence. You are right.
It is a moving story. But this Dona Hoffman, she is too
beautiful. No one is that wonderful. You have been betrayed
by her ego to think that she is some strange, holy, God-filled
creature, and I hereby expose her: She is not wonderful.
NOT. Repeat that 70 times 7. My spirit was not lifted by
the reading of that tome: Truth weighs heavily. I am not
wonderful, and I know.

In Yiddish *goyische mazel* means "Gentile luck,"
undeserved. Therefore—grace, through Jesus Christ, is
goyische mazel. Right?

We have decided to live here another year. There has
been no house for rent in our school district, where the
riots are fewer than anywhere else. In Seattle beatings were
a daily occurrence. My sons escaped many of them, but Mike
was once knifed, Larry's head pushed against a brick wall,
and a lighter put to Dan's nose, burning the mucous lining.
It was not pleasant, and I'd rather live here than return
to that kind of life in a different school area.

> Love surrounds me—
> and I feel it—and know it—
> and return it
>   to you.
> Dona

123

Dear Dona,

If there is any possibility of a "book" to come out of you, the subject is not really you. If there is any glory, it is not really yours, but "your Father's in heaven" (Matt. 5:16). But it may be necessary for people to see you in order to see Him. If you are afraid for that to happen, you may be hiding a great potential light under a bushel! "Not I, but Christ in me," St. Paul would say if anyone began to see something "wonderful" there (Gal. 2:20). And, "By the grace of God I am what I am . . . yet not I, but the grace of God." (1 Cor. 15:10)

So the story is not about you really, nor about me, if anything I have written should be part of it. It is about the grace of God — this unthinkable God of ours, who pours out sufferings so inequitably and with what looks like such thoughtless and loveless and indifferent cruelty, as He did to the Son of His love on Calvary, and as He does to Christ in you — and who by His Spirit through pain and doubt, terror and temptation, still generates His "Yes, Lord." That's what it's all about! And the theme, the very call and reason to put it down somehow with all the investment of love and art of which Dona Hoffman is capable, is what St. Paul puts down for you in 2 Cor. 1:3-7. Read it! There are people out there longing and waiting to be comforted!

"My spirit was not lifted," you say, and, "Truth weighs heavily." Do you understand why? Dona's earthly and visible reality of flesh and sin is getting in the way of God and His miracle, like a dark cloud that shuts out the sun. So you need to learn yet how to see and wonder at God's grace in you. Don't deny me the joy of saying it! Dona, you are very pretty; Dona, you are wonderful; Dona, what a great gift God has given me to know you at least a little! For you are God's, and the glory is God's. If I knew all your faults as Hal is privileged to know them, I would still know them only as Christ knows mine, with perfect and cleansing forgiveness —so that the wonder would be His in you.

Lord Jesus, who came to be Physician for those who suffer, stay close to Dona, love her, lead her tenderly, do with her and get done through her what seems good to you, as she follows you in the Way everlasting.

Much love to you and all,
Paul

Sept. 10, 1973

Dear Paul,

After much rehearsal in *pretending* what my adulthood
should *know*, human love begins once again to seep through
to me, and after that, God's love. Then everything's okay
for a while. Do you understand? I guess it really doesn't
matter if you do or don't, because that's the way it is. No
great blazing conversion, mine: just an agonizing series of
little dots of light, which I must carefully gather and shape
into a very frail understanding.

I wait for God to send another little "dot." He will. But
you must be patient with me. I am a slow gatherer!

"I went down to the potter's house, and there he was
working at his wheel. And the vessel he was making of clay
was spoiled . . . and he reworked it into another vessel,
as it seemed good for the potter to do." (Jer. 18:3, 4)

Centering, being reworked . . .
Dona

P. S. Don't despair. There are some days I truly understand.
In the second volume of "Knock Gently" I could write this:

Reflection while peeling a carrot:
Of course I am wonderful. *God* is
in me! *Kiss me.*

126

Mobile, 11/3/73

Dear Paul,

This week's reflection: The "faith healers" and those
who seek this kind of healing—are they in need, perhaps, of
visible signs as a bridge to the invisible God? And God allows
some of us these signs (even like tongues) to sustain us
awhile and then pushes us beyond healing to desire Him in
His imperceptible totality? But the healers seem mostly
to stop with the signs, and that is why their protest against
suffering and death seems so myopic. Especially in the light
of 2 Cor. 4 and others. Does this line of reasoning make
sense?

You talked to Harold. Thank you. Whatever you said,
he seems more peaceful. He has consistently refused even
to look at my test results, good or bad, or to discuss them.
(But he suffers with me, and he loves the children and
worships the same God as I. I cannot ask for more.)

He pushes for surgery, wants to take the chance. I cower
at the mere thought. My local doctor is convinced it would
be the right thing, but doesn't volunteer. The Seattle doctor
feels he can handle it okay with nitrous oxide and (later)
aspirin. Seems like the whole world is saying, "Have the
surgery, Dona." And when I talk to God about it, He is
silent. As if to say, "It doesn't really matter, you know."

I am a coward. Do you know that? Does anybody? My
faith is small, and my courage is a sickly thing to behold.

Humor is a cover, not a token of bravery. It is not only my body that is contemptible to me!

It's a great relief, a delivering, that God knows my cowardice, all my secret tremblings. And I appreciate your reminder that the resurrection proves how my wretchedness will be a laughing matter.

> Tomorrow is Holy Communion.
> I will be remembering the carrots
> and Ps. 85:10b RSV.
>   Dona

JOURNEY

My soul runs
arms outstretched
    down the corridor to you.

Ah, my feet may stumble
but how my heart can stride!

OTHER MOMENTS

These are the other moments
(the ones they didn't talk about, who've gone
    before)
    which you bear in silence:
your dreams echo your illness
down long dusty corridors
        shouting wave upon wave of accusing sound
and your children file past
        lost and wondering, in gray dusty silence

and the thing that wakes you is a rousing chorus
of Bach
        Come Sweet Death.
It is so beautiful you cannot ignore it
and your children are so lost they can't be
        ignored either.
        You are caught between desires
        to live and to die
    unafraid of either
    but wishing for some sign of the former
        because of the faces that haunt you
        during your sleeping and your waking.

WHAT IS IT LIKE TO DIE SO SLOWLY?

It is living as if life held only hope and promise
  while knowing death is around the next corner.

It is a paradox of wholeness
  while waiting for Completion.

It is being careless of the discomforts
and the inconsistencies of this body
  while regarding it as the Spirit's temple.
It is laughing at life and laughing at death
simultaneously
  while remembering life is a precious, one-time
   gift
  and death's terrors are yet to be experienced.

It is being afraid and trying not to be afraid
  loving and trying not to love too dearly
  giving up, taking on
  hoping
  giving in, letting go
  raging. Silently or aloud. It makes no
   difference.

It is time
  suspended in the night.

Journal

1974 (after surgery)
January 13

Sunday. They have found for me a beautiful gift: a quarter of a child's dose that takes the edge off the pain. I call it my pain-crumb.

January 16

Remembering how I felt, briefly, after surgery: Hey, God, I done good, huh. God wipes the sweat from His brow. The wings of thousands of angels are nearly defeathered from all that watching, that hov'ring over. "You done good, kid," God says, smiling, knowing I know.

January 18

Friday. Discharged from the hospital. Still on catheter, pills, advice, etc. Spent the evening at the motel, letting Harold pack for both of us, trying to overcome pain by watching seagulls and terns, and the comings and goings of the ships on the Sound. Tomorrow, destination: Mobile.

January 19

Saturday.
Amy hugged me, sat on my lap in the small wheelchair, and we cried together. "We sure missed us," I said to her. She nodded, hid her face in my neck, and sobbed and sobbed.

I sit on the lap of God
and cry and cry
    and I do not understand
    except that I love Him
    and wonder what is next.

April 2

I am buried (oh, poor choice of words again) under reams of crumpled paper, dictionaries, file folders, pencils, drawings. Tami approaches quietly, cautiously. "Mama, what is your book about?"

I put down my pencil and wonder with her awhile. "It's about God," I tell her. "It's about how God taps you on the shoulder just when you think He isn't even around. It's about how He pulls you up on His lap and hugs you, and you had been thinking all along that He didn't even notice you. I guess it's just about God caring."

Someone once asked me, "Isn't that the sign of a divided heart?" And I said, "No. It means Jesus gets all the way to the bottom."

134